Masters of Music

ILLUSTRATED BY RICHARD SHIRLEY SMITH

DEBUSSY

Masters of Music

DEBUSSY

Percy M. Young

Ernest Benn · London
David White · New York

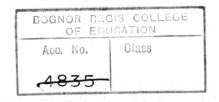
FIRST PUBLISHED 1968
BY ERNEST BENN LIMITED
BOUVERIE HOUSE · FLEET STREET
LONDON · EC4
& DAVID WHITE
66 EAST 55TH STREET · NEW YORK · NY10022

© PERCY M. YOUNG 1968

ILLUSTRATIONS © ERNEST BENN LIMITED 1968

PRINTED IN GREAT BRITAIN

SBN 510-13714-8

LIBRARY OF CONGRESS CATALOG CARD NUMBER
68-9036

Contents

5

Preface

MUSICIANS, like most other people, fall into two groups: on the one hand, those who conform to the social and cultural code of their age; on the other, those who do not. Debussy belonged to the non-conformist group—a situation that may be readily appreciated today. As is usual in such cases he found life difficult. He was not much helped by his family background, nor by his temperament, and for the greater part of his career he was engaged in fighting off attacks both on his music and his morals. At the same time he was trying to earn a living.

Most composers in the course of history were practising musicians, in possession of stipends from public (or from private) offices. In the nineteenth century—an age of commerce—the idea that an artist was not, in the general sense, "a man of the world" was generally accepted. Even artists themselves often tended to subscribe to this idea. Sometimes—as in the cases of Wagner and Liszt—they were able to capitalise on it. Debussy, unfortunately for him, was not.

Now it is seldom that a complete disregard for society goes hand in hand with genius. In the case of Debussy it did. He was, indeed, one of the most original and, to use the commonplace word, inspired composers of the age in which he lived. Unlike those who were famous when he was painfully trying to establish himself—for example, Brahms, Verdi, Tchaikovsky, and Dvořák—he did not summarise the achievements of the past by keeping within sight of the broad tradition. On the contrary, he was one of the principal

architects of the music of the twentieth century. He destroyed existing notions concerning melody, rhythm, harmony, and instrumentation; he pointed out, what was a fresh
thought, that the possibilities of musical sonorities were
endless; he did much to dethrone the myth of "good taste".
This process still continues.

Debussy, however, was a quiet revolutionary, so far as
music was concerned. His works, in comparison with those
of the great composers of the past, are of slender nature,
free from merely rhetorical gestures, often near the edge of
silence. He was the first great composer (with the possible
exception of Chopin) whose reputation depends on a handful
of mostly small-scale pieces.

Debussy, as one should expect from a Frenchman, was
logical. He saw that in the end music was a matter for the
individual, that it was a complex of aural "impressions", and
that by pursuing his own individual aims he was also, in the
long run, giving freedom to others. Whether we like it or
not, Debussy did not hold the classics in conventional regard. It is only by escaping from the bondage of automatic
and exaggerated respect for the classics that we come to
appreciate them. From Debussy we may learn how to make
each musical experience a fresh experience, and how to listen
even to familiar music as if for the first time.

By a strange irony Debussy himself has by now acquired
some of the marks of a classic. His status is assured, his
musical reputation is beyond question, he provides material
for examiners to base solemn questions on, and he qualifies
for this series. And, we may think, he is among the composers whose music may be "understood".

Looking back across fifty years we should be grateful that
this is so. After all, Debussy did not go out of his way to per-

plex his listeners. Quite the reverse, his intention was to clarify. A great master of the pianoforte, and with a sympathy for and understanding of the young, he left us with material on which we may independently start our own enquiry into the nature of his genius. If one plays the pianoforte modestly one may still happily begin with the *Suite bergamasque*, the *Children's Corner*, and the easier among the *Préludes*, and find oneself on the edge of enchantment.

I am grateful to Messrs Durand & Cie and Editions Jean Jobert for permission to quote from Debussy's works, and to Editions Salabert for permission to include an excerpt from the music of Erik Satie.

P. M. Y.

1. *A School of Painters*

ACHILLE CLAUDE DEBUSSY was born on August 22, 1862, in the village, as it was then, of Saint-Germain-en-Laye, a little way outside Paris. His father, Manuel, of peasant stock, who kept a small china shop, was a man whose interests were greater than his means. He read many books, listened to and talked about music, and was a constant play-goer. But a too casual attitude towards his business meant that he was constantly on the edge of poverty. His wife, Victorine, was said to have been nervously highly-strung. This condition was not improved by the task of living with a husband whose words were more telling than his deeds; nor by having five children, for whose maintenance there were uncertain and inadequate means.

It was fortunate that the children had an aunt—their father's sister—who had acquired some wealth, and was also blessed with the spirit of generosity. This aunt, Mme Roustan, offered to take care of the Debussy children. Their mother accepted the offer, except in the case of the eldest. Achille Claude, therefore, became, as it were, an only son — but with a sister and three brothers. Of the younger children one, Eugène, died of meningitis in 1869.

Achille Claude disliked his first name and in later years preferred to place it second and to be known as Claude. Like Peter Tchaikovsky, Debussy was passionately attached to his mother (though he benefited also from his aunt's generosity) and since he never went to school he was much in her company. In so far as he had any primary education he had

11

it from his mother. It is not surprising that he grew up, as would now be thought, with many deficiencies in his academic make-up. To take the obvious point; he was—even when well-known as a composer—bad at spelling. He disliked lessons, and he disliked games. On the other hand he was fascinated by the detail of small ornaments, by pictures, by the magic of butterfly wings. He thought that perhaps he would like to be a painter. In a sense, but not the obvious one, he was.

It is not surprising that a sensitive boy, whose thoughts so often centred on details of design and on the interplay of colours, and who was French, should think at that time of becoming a painter. For, just then, there was a great school of painters—the most notable of modern times—active in France.

Théodore Rousseau (1812–67) was a master of landscape, who conveyed through the boldness of his work and an eye for detail, the vigour and the variety of nature. Rousseau, who was bitterly opposed by conventional artists, rejected sentimentality. So too did Jean Millet (1814–75), who was the first French painter of that age to show peasants as they were and not as they were romantically supposed to be. Eugène Boudin (1825–98) was attracted by the sea and the sky and his analytical eye taught him that there was in these elements an infinite wealth of colour—which he was able to transfer to canvas.

These painters inspired others to paint what they saw, to be "realistic", to be truthful. Gustave Courbet (1819–77), whose progressive tendencies in art were linked to a generally radical outlook, once refused to paint angels when asked to do so by a patron. "What I have not seen," he said, "I cannot paint."

In 1874 a particular group of painters was achieving fame through notoriety. In that year Edouard Manet (1823–83), Claude Monet (1840–1926), and Auguste Renoir (1841–1919), as well as others, had pictures refused for the official, Salon Exhibition in Paris. One of Monet's paintings, a study of sunrise, was called an *Impression*. Because these pictures were particularly disliked by the conservative critics, and because this one in particular caught their anger and ridicule, the group of painters to which Monet belonged was dubbed the "Impressionists". A hundred years later pictures by these painters are shown in reproduction on almost every school-room wall, and originals are sold for sums of money which the painters themselves would not have believed to exist. In 1967 a painting by Monet fetched nearly £600,000 in London.

"Impressionism" is an important term, not only in respect of painting, but also of music, and, to a certain extent, of literature. Before the style was established painters (and other artists) tried to convey the "meaning" of their subjects —meaning in this sense being related to narrative. The Impressionist painters, realising that pictures cannot tell stories, acted on the principle that it was only what was *seen* that was important to the artist. Therefore they concentrated on the nature of colour, which, as the scientists of the nineteenth century proved, was both more complex and more simple than was believed. More complex because the colours the eye recognises are ever changing, according to the vibrations of light at any moment. More simple, because of the possibility of being able to break down colour into its basic "pure" tones, as by means of the spectroscope.

The Impressionists were concerned, as it were, with the freedom and the rhythmic quality of colour. They also tried to represent scenes (or subjects) as a whole, as they were taken in by the eye at one glance (or impression), and not by studying details and patiently adding them one by one long after the scene had changed. To some extent these painters took painting in the direction of music, and in looking at an Impressionist painting from a musical angle one may feel that colours have been treated as are the separate tone-qualities in a musical work. Moreover, one may say that such a painting as Monet's famous "Sunrise" has a sense of movement, of rhythm.

The coming together of music and painting under the general heading of Impressionism was brought about by Claude Debussy. At the back of his mind there was the slender ambition he had once had to be a painter; even though this was never a very serious ambition.

It was Debussy's aunt, Mme Roustan, who first discovered that he had musical aptitude. She arranged for him to have piano lessons. By good fortune Debussy met a former pupil of Frédéric Chopin, a Mme de Fleurville, who having heard Claude play offered to give him lessons. She was certain that his gifts were such that he should aim at becoming a musician. Mme de Fleurville's daughter, Mathilde, became the wife of Paul Verlaine (1844–96), a famous poet with whom Debussy was later associated.

Debussy's father had once thought that his son should join the navy. It is worth noting that one of Debussy's most famous works is called *La Mer* (*The Sea*)—that when he composed it he reminded a friend that he had once thought that he might become a sailor. The idea of a musical career, however, seemed a much better one when it was suggested to him. The elder Debussy, with artistic inclinations that were never developed, looked forward, perhaps, to the realisation of his own unspoken ambitions through his son. For a start he made Claude practise the piano for several hours a day.

2. *The Importance of Ear-training*

IN FORMER TIMES musicians, whether performers or composers, were created by a process of specialisation that is now only permissible in respect of sport. For the most part the great musicians of the past were put through rigorous, often exclusive, courses of training almost from infancy. In the nineteenth century this principle was applied less frequently. Composers like Berlioz, Mendelssohn, Schumann, Wagner, and Tchaikovsky, all enjoyed a liberal form of education and each of these could have successfully competed in other fields than that of music.

In the case of Debussy, however, the case was otherwise. His formal education narrowed down to the study of music, which from the age of eleven he underwent at the Paris Conservatoire. This was, in part, a matter of economics. In contrast to the composers mentioned above Debussy was brought up in near poverty. In his father's view his marked talent for music was the one way of escaping from poverty. Manuel Debussy, hoping that his son would succeed where he himself had failed, anticipated the day when Claude would be a famous pianist.

The career of a genius is strewn with as many failures as successes (a fact which is encouraging to the rest of us, but one that is often overlooked) and Debussy was no exception to the general rule. He spent eleven years at the Conservatoire and when he won prizes they were second rather than

first prizes. There was, however, one exception. At the age of fifteen Debussy was top of his class for *solfège*.

Solfège, an extension of the classical Italian method of training singers, was basically a system of ear-training. The Paris Conservatoire was famous for its courses in *solfège*, and students were given extremely strict instruction. They were taught to recognise sounds, to analyse them in melodic and harmonic contexts, and in the complex interweaving of separate parts in counterpoint; they were taught to read music at sight, and to be able to transpose from one key to another at the keyboard. Debussy, analytical by nature, benefited much from the course in *solfège*, as may be appreciated from the precision and clarity that was to mark his compositions.

Debussy's teacher in *solfège* was Albert Lavignac (1846–1916), otherwise known as the editor of an Encyclopedia of Music. His piano teacher was Antoine Marmontel (1816–98), author of several books on piano technique. Marmontel, a specialist in his own field, appreciated his pupils when they showed a similar sense of dedication. Debussy did not. The relationship between master and pupil, therefore, was not particularly close. Nor was it between Debussy and his harmony teacher, Emile Durand (1830–1903), who was, he thought, interested only in the dry bones of music. All these professors tended to hold out to their pupils the standard "classical" works, indicating (as sometimes still happens) that to attempt to compose in the light of their existence was an act of impiety.

Debussy, who said that he particularly disliked the music of Beethoven, preferred to rely on his own judgement. He also considered that the music of the present deserved as much attention as that of the past. On this account he appeared to his teachers as rebellious. But with this show of independence he moved into the best classical company. In one way or another all the great composers were rebels.

There were other reasons than musical that were liable in those days to affect the taste of a young Frenchman. The memory of the defeat of France in the Franco-Prussian War of 1870 was fresh enough to create some resistance to German music, just as it was a stimulus to a patriotic regard for French music. The dominant figure in French music, of course, was Hector Berlioz (1803–69), for whose music Debussy had a high regard. Other figures of importance during Debussy's student days were Edouard Lalo (1823–92), a composer of Spanish descent, Jules Massenet (1842–1912), and César Franck (1822–90), Belgian by birth. In one way or another all three composers moved away from the accepted norm of German techniques, experimenting with rhythms, tone-colours, and harmonies, but not far enough for the more radically minded young. During this same period *Opéra Comique*, or operetta, and ballet flourished; the masters of the one were Jacques Offenbach (1819–80) and Alexandre Lecocq (1832–1918), and of the other Léo Delibes (1836–91), whose *Sylvia*, first produced in 1876, was particularly admired by Tchaikovsky.

3. *Mme von Meck and Mme Vasnier*

IN THE SUMMER OF 1880, by a curious quirk of fate, Debussy became closely acquainted with the music of Tchaikovsky. The patroness of Tchaikovsky, Mme Nadezhda von Meck, a wealthy widow with a passion for music and especially that of Tchaikovsky (whom she never met), applied to the Paris Conservatoire for a student who could act as music tutor to her daughters during the summer holidays. The authorities of the Conservatoire recommended Debussy, who thus unexpectedly found himself travelling to Switzerland to meet his temporary employer and her children.

One of the children of Mme von Meck remembered, and, later, wrote of the arrival of the young Frenchman. He was small in stature, dark in colouring, vivacious and prone to fix a nickname on each of his new acquaintances. He was also inclined to be sarcastic.

It was a beautiful summer. Debussy enjoyed the luxury of life with the von Meck family — Mme von Meck spared no expense to make her guests comfortable — and went with them from Switzerland to Italy. After staying in Rome the party moved on to Florence, where Debussy not only taught his pupils (falling in love with one of them), but also played the piano in the chamber music recitals that his employer liked to arrange.

Mme von Meck had a passion not only for music in general but also for certain musicians in particular. Tchaikovsky was at the top of the list, and one of Debussy's special tasks was to make a piano duet arrangement of some of the dances from *Swan Lake*. Mme von Meck also had a high regard for the works of Mily Balakirev (1837–1910), one of the leading figures of the Russian nationalist school. She shared all her enthusiasms with her young protégé and if he did not always see eye to eye with her he at least became aware of the wider field of music. At the Conservatoire in Paris Debussy had been introduced to the music of Wagner (which came to exert a strong influence in France) by Lavignac. Mme von Meck introduced Debussy to Wagner personally, in Venice, in 1880.

Debussy was reluctant to go back to Paris, but his tutors refused his request to interrupt his studies in order to stay on with the von Meck family. However, in the following year he was able to go to stay with them in Russia, where he not only increased his knowledge of Russian music but also of Russian life. Mme von Meck's son, Vladimir, knew the best places in Moscow where the young could live it up. Debussy was not averse from accompanying him on his nights out. He went back to France, therefore, with copies of music by Alexander Borodin (1813–87) and Nikolai Rimsky-Korsakov (1844–1908) but also with the tunes he had picked up from his congenial visits to the cabaret clubs.

Mme von Meck called Debussy her "Little Frenchman", and she gave him the stimulus to believe in himself as a composer. He wrote songs, piano pieces, some chamber music, and a symphony. The last work was dedicated to his patroness, and one movement, arranged for piano duet, which was discovered in manuscript in a Russian collection has been published by the Soviet State Publishing Company. A few songs (one dedicated to Alexander von Meck) of the period were also published.

It is often said that travel broadens the mind. That, of course, depends. To travel for the sake of travel accomplishes nothing. The real value comes when the traveller learns to live with other people, of a different culture or tradition, and to absorb the ideas and ideals that are to be encountered. As a young student, Debussy, with practically no academic background (other than musical) and a sketchy acquaintance with what in polite circles passes as culture, was at a disadvantage. His friendship with the von Mecks introduced him to new values, as well as to new people, and broadened his outlook and sympathies. But he was still a student, and he had his course to attend to in Paris.

After his first summer with the von Mecks, Debussy joined the composition class of Ernest Guiraud (1837–92), a composer of operas and a friend of Georges Bizet (1838–75). Although now largely forgotten Guiraud was an accomplished musician. He composed recitatives for Bizet's *Carmen*, orchestrated *The Tales of Hoffmann* of Offenbach, and wrote a text-book on instrumentation. As his career suggests eh was broad-minded. As the teacher of Debussy, he needed to be.

For a teacher who wanted a quiet life, Debussy was not the ideal pupil. He was easily offended, not a very good mixer, inclined to bursts of anger or to sulky moods, a bad loser at cards, and somewhat uncouth. On the other hand, he could be charming to those whom he liked, and amusing. His humour, however, always had a sharp edge, and he was well-known for his skill in caricature. He would often entertain himself, and others, by musical caricatures extemporised at the piano. He was especially inclined to parody the music of Wagner, and of this pastime there is an example in the "Golliwog's Cakewalk" of later date. This is the passage from

Ex.1

a) *Wagner: Tristan*

b) *Debussy: Golliwog's Cakewalk*

Wagner's *Tristan and Isolde*, followed by Debussy's version (which must, of course, be heard in its context).

Against the *Tristan* theme Debussy puts a lugubrious bass, and then follows it with short, sharp, chords, made spicey by the "crush" notes of the right hand.

At other times when his friends heard the young Debussy extemporise they were amazed at the new kinds of chords and harmonic progressions that appeared—all against the "rules". There were some professors at the Conservatoire who took a very poor view of Debussy. He was noted as a "rebel". Fortunately there were some people who realised that he had great talent, and among these was the best student of his time at the Conservatoire—Paul Vidal (1863–1931). Through Vidal's friendship Debussy obtained a post as accompanist to a choral society, of which the president was Charles Gounod (1818–93), then one of the most influential of French musicians. He was also recommended as accompanist to a well-known singing-teacher, Mme Moreau-Sainti. Among her pupils was Mme Vasnier, the young and attractive wife of an elderly architect.

Members of certain professions tend to attract the interest and affection of women. History shows a long procession of ladies who have been captivated (sometimes against their better judgement) by musicians. Mme Vasnier belongs to this class. Attracted by Debussy's evident, but not always appreciated, gifts, and affected by his poverty and by the fact that his parents took little interest in him, she began by taking pity on him. She gave him the run of her house, and of her villa in the country. Her husband introduced him to the works of two famous contemporary poets, Verlaine and Stéphane Mallarmé (1842–98). Settings of poems by these, as well as other, poets, appeared during the last three years of Debussy's student days, to be sung by Mme Vasnier, to whom they were dedicated. Through Mme Vasnier's influence a *Nocturne and Scherzo* for violin and piano was played at a concert given by the violinist Maurice Thiéberg in 1882.

Like other benefactresses Mme Vasnier's feelings underwent a change as she came to know her protégé better and better. She fell in love with him.

In the meantime Debussy was aiming at the highest award given by the French Institute. This was the *Prix de Rome* in music (there were similar awards for painting, sculpture, engraving, and architecture), established by the Academy of Fine Arts, a branch of the Institute, in 1803. On the list of musicians who gained the *Prix de Rome* were the names of Berlioz, Bizet, and Massenet. The winner in 1883 was

Debussy's friend, Vidal, Debussy being runner-up. In the following year, however, he was successful, his strongest supporter on the jury being Charles Gounod.

The work which Debussy submitted for this test was a dramatic cantata, *L'Enfant prodigue* (*The Prodigal Son*). Having gained the prize on which he had set his heart he prepared to leave for Italy. By the terms of the prize successful candidates were given the opportunity to study in Rome, for a period of three, sometimes four, years, at the expense of the French government. Curiously, but not uncharacteristically, Debussy was not at all sure that he wanted to go to Rome. At the end of January 1885, however, he arrived there, and went into the room waiting for him at the Villa Medici.

[handwritten margin note: 1884 Debussy won Prix de Rome]

4. *Composer in the Making*

SOME YEARS BEFORE, in the company of the von Mecks, Debussy had seen the outside of the Villa Medici. One of the von Meck children, indeed, had said to him: "You will live there one day." Now that day had come the young composer was thoroughly miserable. He had to share a room with five other students. It was, into the bargain, a dirty room. The weather was bad, the students unfriendly, and his health (he said) was bad. Many nineteenth-century composers, particularly Robert Schumann and Tchaikovsky, displayed similar aversions, and complained about their health.

These aversions and complaints, often amounting to self-pity, had been accepted by those of a romantic disposition as the marks of the Romantic, if not of an "artistic" temperament. Where they exist, they are, more often, symptoms of a discontent with the place of the individual (in this case, the artist) in society. The nineteenth century, an age of commerce and of industrial expansion, was less kind to the arts than the eighteenth century. Partly because of this, partly because of a growing technical crisis within music itself, the nineteenth-century composer was often aware of a sense of frustration. In the case of Debussy this has already shown itself in his avowed distaste for the "classics" and for the principles of composition accepted by the public, critics and composers (for the most part) alike. And here he was in Rome, unhappy, and uncertain.

Debussy spent two years in Rome. He was fortunate to the extent that he was able to hear a good deal of music that

was new to him, and to meet some of the leading musicians of the day. During this period he studied the organ works of Bach, and the scores of Wagner's operas, especially of *Lohengrin*, the most lyrical in spirit of Wagner's works, and *Tristan and Isolde*. First performed in 1865 this work then represented the last stages in the progress of harmonic development over a period of 250 years. In *Tristan* concepts of fixed tonal centres no longer obtained, for the harmonies of the work were in a continual state of flux. This begins to appear even in the three-bar quotation from the beginning of the Prelude on p. 25. Many composers noted the fact, but some preferred to shut their eyes to it, and went on composing as though *Tristan* had not happened. Debussy was too honest to do this. He realised that a new attitude to musical composition was needed, and new principles of composition. One day he went into a small church in Rome and heard music by the sixteenth-century composers, Lassus and Palestrina. This was a gateway into a new world of sound, and he was entranced by the inter-weaving of the vocal parts. Studies in academic counterpoint he had found depressing. Now listening to music that was contrapuntal, rather than looking at counterpoint that often was not music, he recognised that it offered one way towards freedom.

This, too, was an obsession (as it is with most young people). Writing to M. Vasnier one day he thought it unlikely that his tutors in Paris would think much of the music he was composing at the time. "But," he went on, "I'm too fond of my freedom . . . [and] I cannot write the kind of music they would approve."

Debussy, having met one great master of opera—Wagner—now had the opportunity to meet the only other of that age who enjoyed comparable esteem—Giuseppe Verdi

(1813–1901). He was introduced to Verdi by the librettist and composer, Arrigo Boito (1842–1918), and to Franz Liszt (1811–86) at the house of Giovanni Sgambati (1841–1914), a Roman pupil of Liszt and a well-known composer.

Debussy was fortunate to hear Liszt, the greatest pianist of the age, play. Out of courtesy to his young visitor Liszt, with Sgambati as his partner, played the *Variations on a theme of Beethoven* (op. 35) for two pianos by Camille Saint-Saëns (1835–1921). Debussy remembered this as one of the greatest moments in his life. It was also the last time that Liszt played to anyone in Rome.

Liszt was not only a great pianist, but also a great composer. Not only that, but he was a great innovator. So far as the technique of piano music was concerned, he developed through new figurations a new sense of brilliance, which influenced many composers, in particular Maurice Ravel (1875–1937), whose name is so often coupled with that of Debussy. Liszt also had a genius for using the tone-colours of the piano to convey atmosphere, and so, in due course, did Debussy. Recognising that old methods of harmony were on the way out Liszt experimented—with Hungarian, or gipsy scales, on the one hand, and with whole tone scales and the old church scales, or modes, on the other. The revolutions of style for which Debussy was to become famous were already in the air. This is always the case. Change in music is more gradual than sometimes is made to appear. The innovator, as a rule, is in fact usually giving fuller expression to ideas already in circulation, but combining them together in a convincing manner.

In addition to coming into contact with new music Debussy also became aware of new literary developments while he was in Rome. The newest movement in French

c

poetry was defined as *Symbolism*, and its chief exponents were Verlaine and Mallarmé. After the Franco-Prussian War of 1870 there was a craving for pleasure, for liveliness, for colour, in Paris. The music of Wagner appeared to many Frenchmen as the very height of sensuous pleasure and it became the avowed aim of men of letters to return to poetry as much as they could of the values of music. Thus the poetry of Verlaine and Mallarmé is more convincing by reason of its sound than of its sense. In our own day something of a similar nature is to be found in the poems of Dylan Thomas.

Debussy returned to France in 1887 with little in the way

of composition to show for his abbreviated studies in Rome, and nothing that was likely to attract the attention of the musicians of Paris. Not content merely to write music for the sake of writing it, he was still looking for an individual path to pursue. Since the general run of musicians were conservative in attitude he avoided their company and sought that of writers. Among them there were many who at least were idealists, with stimulating and progressive views. Debussy was an occasional guest at the home of Mallarmé, but, shy and reticent, he could hardly have been described as the life and soul of the party. He made one friend, Pierre Louÿs (1870–1925), poet and novelist, whose sympathy and support was for a number of years of great importance.

The Symbolists approved the music of Wagner, because it appealed directly to the senses. Debussy was a keen enough Wagnerian, but some way this side of idolatry. He decided that he must go to Bayreuth to hear Wagner's music under the ideal conditions of the Festival Theatre. But first he went to Vienna, where he met Brahms—the greatest symphonist of the age. After appearing less than pleased to meet a young and unknown Frenchman Brahms was most hospitable. He entertained Debussy at his house, went with him to a performance of Bizet's *Carmen*, spoke on the theme of national greatness in respect of Germany and France, and wished his young visitor well. At Bayreuth in 1888 and 1889 Debussy saw *Parsifal*, *The Mastersingers*, and *Tristan and Isolde*—three strongly contrasted works. Debussy admired the music, but felt that its textures were too complicated, and that the voice parts were obscured by the richness and variety of the orchestration.

In 1889 Debussy encountered a musical idiom that was the complete antidote to that of Germany. In that year at the

International Exhibition in Paris concerts were given by many national teams of folk-music, from Asia, from Africa, and from the farther away countries of Europe. Debussy listened to the gipsies of Hungary, the peasants from Romania, and to the *gamelan* musicians from Java (Indonesia). The Javanese musicians played the *rabab* (a kind of two-stringed viol), the *suling* (a bamboo flute), the *selompret* (of the oboe family), the *chemelpung* (related to the cither group), and a large variety of percussion instruments, a number of which were gongs of different sizes. Having heard this kind of music, partly extemporised, in scales unfamiliar to western ears, and brilliantly exciting and beautiful in its range of tone-colours, Debussy realised that in order to fulfil his ideals he must forget the sense of superiority inherent in western European music and keep in view the wider horizons. Potentially, *all* sounds, not only some, were the basic vocabulary from which the composer must draw.

Unknown to him another musician in Paris was thinking along similar lines. This was Erik Satie (1866–1925), who after one year at the Conservatoire forsook the customary paths of respectability and earned a meagre living by playing the piano in cafés and by composing songs for the music-hall. In 1887 Satie published a set of three *Sarabandes* and in 1888 a set of pieces entitled *Gymnopédies*. The latter title was derived from a Greek word and suggested the ideal of physical beauty, demonstrated in dancing and athletic sports, so dear to the Greeks of classical times. Satie's music was the very opposite to the styles current in the 1880's. It was light, delicate, with melodies suspended, as it were, in mid-air; and with a harmonic background that, making use of sharp, but discreet, dissonances, owed next to nothing to the rules of the text-books. (Ex. 2) This is an idiom which is familiar

Ex. 2

to those who are acquainted with the music of Debussy and Ravel, even if not with that of Satie himself. That this is so explains the enthusiasm with which both Debussy and Ravel welcomed Satie's music. In acknowledgement of his early appreciation of Satie Debussy orchestrated two of the *Gymnopédies* in 1897.

The two men met for the first time in 1891 and they remained on terms of intimacy for many years. Satie wrote of the first meeting: "The moment I saw him, I felt drawn to him and wished I might live at his side for ever. And for thirty years I was fortunate enough to see my wish fulfilled." Debussy and Satie discussed Impressionism and Symbolism. Satie was strongly anti-Wagner and in proposing that French music should spring from French (and not German) roots said, "Why shouldn't we make use of the methods employed by Claude Monet, Cézanne, Toulouse-Lautrec, etc." They also talked about opera, and on his side of the conversation Satie brought together the principles both of Symbolism (as expressed in literature) and Impressionism (as expressed in painting). In suggesting the exclusion of mere busy-ness from music he came very near to describing the music of Debussy.

"There is," he said, "no need for the orchestra to grimace when a character comes on the stage. Do the trees in the scenery grimace? What we have to do is to create a musical scenery, a musical atmosphere in which the characters move and talk . . ."

Satie was busy on an opera based on a play by the Belgian writer, Maurice Maeterlinck (1862–1949). An imaginative, mystical, writer, Maeterlinck made a strong appeal to musicians—among them Paul Dukas (1865–1935), Arnold Schoenberg (1874–1951) and Debussy. In 1892 the last named bought a copy of the recently published *Pelléas et Mélisande*, and knew at once that that was the opera he wanted to compose. What Satie had said about the nature of opera was a great encouragement. The composition of this opera took ten years.

While he is composing a composer has to live. Often, as in the case of Debussy, it was a hand-to-mouth existence. He made arrangements and transcriptions for publishing houses: played the piano—usually excerpts from Wagner—at musical evenings; played the musical illustrations for lectures. He wrote songs—to poems by Verlaine, Charles Baudelaire (1821–67), and Mallarmé, and piano pieces, including the two graceful *Arabesques* and the *Petite suite* for piano duet. In 1893 he made a slight impression on the musical public when his cantata for women's voices and orchestra, *The Blessed Damosel*, and a string quartet were performed at concerts of the Société Nationale.

The former work, based on a French version of the poem by Dante Gabriel Rossetti, is a translation of the spirit of the English pre-Raphaelite school into terms of music, and as such is highly colourful. It is languid music—far from the energetic character of "symphonic" music—and in its languorousness showed a new kind of musical thought. It was not greatly appreciated, however, and by one critic was dismissed as "decadent". In respect of the String Quartet, now regarded as one of Debussy's finest works, some thought it was influenced by the idiom of the contemporary Russian school, others by the *gamelan* music of Java. A year later the work by which Debussy is now best known, *L'Après-midi d'un faune*, was performed for the first time.

Again, there was little attention paid to the music—what praise there was was luke-warm—but the composer, with three substantial works behind him, and others on the way, was launched. He now had confidence in himself, and knew where he was going.

5. *A Matter of Style*

DURING THE SECOND HALF of the nineteenth century the composer who aimed at success in the worldly sense (that is, in the sense understood by the majority of people) needed to come to terms with middle-class society. At all times a composer is anything but a free agent; he depends for his livelihood on the "patron" (i.e. the person or public who pays for the music). A patron may be a single person, or a body of people; for instance, the prince on the one hand, or the Church, or the State, on the other. In the second part of the nineteenth century the individual patron counted for little, while organised patronage took its chance in the open market, and, being subject to the rough laws of supply and demand, was, more than ever before, conditioned by public taste and fashion.

The market for music then became a mass market, and the prudent musician learned to exploit it. The demand was for familiar works, for the unadventurous stuck to the principle: what we know we like. Then the classical composers (being dead they did not have to be paid) were more and more firmly established in the general repertoire. For a composer to depart from using the kinds of sound combinations sanctified by the classics, and by the theoreticians who had made a minor industry out of the exposition of the "rules", was thought to be improper. It was, however, thought not disagreeable to organise music for large-scale forces. Wagner gradually sailed into popularity because of the way in which he used enormous forces, and Richard Strauss (1864–1949)

38

also achieved early fame for the same reason. Brahms, Dvořák, and Tchaikovsky, swept across Europe, because they appeared to observe sufficient of the classical precepts (i.e. in the way of symphony and concerto), and to use instrumental (and vocal) resources in a manner that was not too way-out.

This, of course, is reducing the situation to terms which are, in the long run, too simple, for each of the composers named was in some way a pioneer of musical thought. But not to the extent that Debussy was.

Debussy not only attacked the citadels of convention, he quietly set about dismantling them, stone by stone. He defended the right of music to exist in its own right, and not as an elaboration of narrative, nor as the consequence of observing set principles of structure. For him the experience of music, the impression it made on the senses, was all that mattered. Tonality was unimportant; the accepted patterns of rhythm and metre were irrelevant; formal procedures were a hindrance.

The Blessed Damosel has none of the energy associated with the so-called "oratorio" style. It seems, like Rossetti's poem, to float in mid-air. In this work Debussy showed the results of his Wagnerian interests in the use of a motiv that, in different shapes, appears in different sections of the work. (This is the principle of *Leitmotiv*.) Because of its atmosphere—in general, "religious"—*The Blessed Damosel* was not ungenerously received by César Franck and his disciples.

A string quartet, unlike a work with religious associations (however vague), is not able to rely on an already existing atmosphere; it must create its own. This is precisely what Debussy's String Quartet did. As in *The Blessed Damosel* the composer used a *Leitmotiv*. This is shown at the beginning of the work as follows:

Ex.3

In this form it will be noticed that while the key signature is that of G minor, the passage does not *sound* as though it belongs to that key. In fact, Debussy has gone back to one of the medieval modes for the outline of the melody and has derived the chords (note the A flat in the cello part), broadly speaking, from the content of the mode. This represents a denial of the importance of major-minor tonality and all that it stood for. The rejection of harmonic principles is carried a good deal further in the Quartet, for while "chords" are rarely of the order of common, or commonplace, chords, the manner in which set tonal centres are avoided represents a much more notable departure from what was thought to be acceptable in 1893.

The primacy of an elaborate code of key relationships was at that time regarded almost as sacred. So too was the idea that musical themes should "develop". Debussy's Quartet is a series of gestures, in which the main motiv frequently appears but only to disappear as soon as it has been encountered, and of delicate effects of sonority. In short, Debussy uses the four stringed instruments to convey impressions, and not to conduct a conversation. (That a string quartet was a kind of conversation, in which one instrument took up ideas from another and discussed them, derives from an early description of the procedures of Josef Haydn.)

L'Après-midi d'un faune, one of the most famous of Debussy's works, is a miniature of extreme delicacy. The title of Mallarmé's poem, which stimulated the composition, suggests something exotic (for who knows where and how fauns spend their afternoons?) and, at the same time, an atmosphere of complete relaxation. There is a pagan element inherent in the title—and even more in Mallarmé's words. Debussy aimed at collecting together the ideas of the exotic and the pleasurable into a sequence of sounds that encouraged the listener to *feel* rather than to *think*. The score is a masterpiece of subtle instrumentation, in which the quality of the sounds is more effective, and so intended, than the formal activity of the melodic and harmonic elements. Melody, in fact, dissolves into this kind of vaporous trail, the intervals used (mostly, but not all, semitones) destroying a fixed sense of key.

Ex.4

This, with the contour quite freed from the demands of tonality, and definitive rhythm structures, is the beginning of a new type of melody. The whole piece is more significant, as heralding a period in which, in instrumental music, melody is not necessary at all. The spirit of this music spills over into Debussy's song, *Le Faune*, a setting of a poem by Verlaine.

Nothing is ever quite new. Debussy, as many other musicians, was able to appreciate that Wagner had brought tonality to a point of no return, since in his later works divisions between immediately recognisable keys had ceased to exist. The leading Russian nationalist composers, Debussy being particularly aware of the innovations of Modeste Mussorgsky (1839–81), had broken away from the hard-and-fast conventions of melodic design and formal procedure.

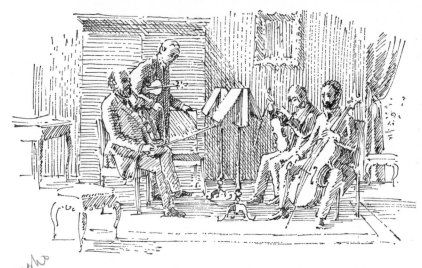

Debu. brought style together

Debussy, however, was the first composer to put together the many revolutionary ideas that were in the air and to shape them into a new and comprehensive style.

The distinguishing feature of western European music of the period between 1650 and 1900 is the harmonic system. Nowhere else in the world at any time has music been so powerfully conditioned by harmonic considerations. Harmony is, of course, not the most important part of music — though, from the reading of text-books, one may often be misled into believing that it is. This is why the coming of "modern music" is often interpreted in terms of revolt against a harmonic system. Debussy, in 1889, stated quite simply that the keyboard octave could be divided into 12 semitones and that "with them one can make any scale one wishes". He went on, in the course of the same conversation with his teacher, Ernest Guiraud, to say that out of the same notes one could make "ambiguous chords, that belong to as many keys as one likes." He further spoke of the merit of "incomplete chords" and "floating intervals".

Something of what Debussy thus defined existed in the medieval background of European music, in the works of the French and Flemish masters of the fifteenth and sixteenth centuries. Otherwise there was folk-music — not that of self-conscious collectors, but of the lively and varied traditions of, for instance, the *gamelan* musicians of the Far East.

Style is the result of a conscious assessment of, and selection from, various methods of expression. The composer — like the painter, the novelist, or the poet, uses those methods, or adopts those attitudes, which seem most congenial to him. At the same time there are unconscious forces at work. A German composer may adopt French methods, or a Frenchman may adopt German methods; but the music of the former (if worth anything at all, and not merely a parody) will retain traits that are recognisably German, just as that of the latter will stand out by reason of its French characteristics. Such characteristics are nothing to do with the rules of music, but spring from the attitude to life of a community. In brief, French thought across the ages is distinguished by its love of clarity, brevity, and logic.

Debussy was a French composer thinking about music in

a French way, and not a French composer who thought it politic to try to think in a German way. After all, the nineteenth century was an age of nationalists, and after 1876 it became a matter of principle in France to emphasise the Frenchness of things. Debussy was not in the narrow sense a nationalist composer; but he could hardly avoid showing some of the attributes of those who were. The aims of the nationalists in many European countries, and of Debussy, were the same: to achieve independence.

6. *The New Music*

ONE MUSICIAN who was greatly impressed by the music and the ideals of Debussy was the Belgian violinist Eugène Ysaÿe (1858–1931), whose quartet gave the first performance of Debussy's String Quartet. During the next year the composer was busy with a new project, a set of pieces for violin and orchestra, and he intended them for Ysaÿe. He wrote to Ysaÿe informing him that the pieces in process of being written were of an experimental nature. The orchestra for the first was to consist of strings only; for the second, flutes, horns, trumpets, and two harps; for the third, the two previous groups together. The work was to correspond to a painter's attempt to explore the possible combinations to be obtained from one colour. In this case, said Debussy, the colour was grey.

The master of such tones so far as painting was concerned was the American-European artist James McNeill Whistler (1834–1903) with whom Debussy had become acquainted in Paris, and whose art was much applauded by Baudelaire. The title which Debussy gave to his three pieces was one which Whistler used to describe his night pictures—*Nocturnes*. (The title was already familiar to musicians through the piano pieces called *Nocturnes* of both John Field (1782–1837) and Frédéric Chopin (1810–49).) Debussy began these pieces for violin and orchestra, but after two or three years he abandoned this idea and scored *Nocturnes* for orchestra alone.

The first movement of *Nocturnes* is "Nuages" ("Clouds")

45

— an impression of the "changeless aspect of the sky and the slow, solemn movement of the clouds, fading away in grey tones, lightly touched with white." "Fêtes", which follows, is as of a festival at night-time, with the animation of the scene moved not only by the natural rhythm of the music but also by the hidden rhythm concentrated in the interplay of the points of instrumental colours. In this connection one sees "rhythm" as when, in painting, one refers to the "movement" or "pattern" of the colours on the canvas. In "Sirènes", the final piece, in which Debussy catches the mood of the sea and the mysterious voice-sounds of the legendary Sirens, a choir of women's voices is introduced; but the voices, regarded as instruments, being without words, are dehumanised and blend into and enhance the orchestral sonorities.

While working at *Nocturnes* Debussy was also busy with his opera *Pelléas et Mélisande*, in which Ysaÿe was also greatly interested. He had other plans, as for a setting of *Willow Wood*, another poem by Rossetti, and for a ballet on the subject of the mythical Greek shepherd and shepherdess Daphnis and Chloe. Neither of these plans was fulfilled. *Willow Wood* was set to music some ten years later by Ralph Vaughan Williams (1872–1958) and it is interesting to notice how, in this work written soon after a visit to France for consultations with Maurice Ravel, he showed the influence of Debussy. The story of Daphnis and Chloe was the basis of a ballet, and one of the most famous works, of Ravel.

Debussy's views on music and any analysis of his methods should not be allowed to hide the simplicity of his philosophy. The aim of music—and of any other art—was to give pleasure. Primarily this meant pleasure to the senses. He

was not, as a musician, concerned to improve people's morals
nor to impress them with religious or any other kind of doc-
trines. In his relative detachment from social and political
affairs, and his determination to live an independent life of
pleasure, he followed the habits of painters and writers in
France who were his contemporaries. He was an atheist; he
had expensive tastes; he had little sense of handling money.
His hopes of earning a livelihood were often dashed by the
impractical way in which he set about realising them.

For at least two hundred years European musicians had
believed that so far as they were concerned the streets of
London were paved with gold. Debussy had been to London
as a boy (he had heard a performance of *H.M.S.Pinafore*, an
operetta by W. S. Gilbert and A. S. Sullivan). In 1887 he
had tried to sell *The Blessed Damosel* to the publishing house
of Novello. Ten years later he investigated the possibilities of
London once more. During this visit he was introduced by
Saint-Saëns to Hubert Parry (1848–1918), Director of the
Royal College of Music, Professor of Music at Oxford
University, and the most influential musician in the country.
But Parry had two interests in music: the German tradition
and the English tradition. These left no room for any particular enthusiasm for French music; certainly not for that of
a young composer who not only broke some of the rules, but
all of them. Debussy's visit to London was not a success.

Since his student days Debussy had had a succession of
girl-friends. During the time he was composing *Pelléas et
Mélisande* and *Nocturnes* he acquired a new one, Rosalie
Texier, a pretty dress-maker. In 1899 he married her, after
first giving a piano lesson on the morning of the wedding-day
in order to be able to pay for the wedding-breakfast.

In 1900 the first two movements of Nocturnes were given

D

at one of the concerts of the series instituted by Charles Lamoureux (1834–99), and, being received with acclamation, were repeated during the following season, together with the final movement. At an International Exhibition held in Paris, also in 1900, performances of *The Blessed Damosel*, the String Quartet, and other pieces by Debussy, were given with official blessing. He had arrived. In 1901 he was appointed music critic of a Paris journal, which gave him a platform from which to express his views otherwise than through his music. His critical essays, as well as the views on music expressed in his letters, are of great interest in understanding the principles that came to distinguish twentieth-century from nineteenth-century music. In his first essay for the *Revue blanche* Debussy wrote: "I will try to discover the forces that have brought works of art into being, which I think to be more worth-while than taking them to pieces like an old watch."

7. *Scandal*

THE HISTORY OF MUSIC is strewn with memorial-stones, each of which marks some kind of terminus. Debussy is accepted as a musician of a new dispensation; and that we may now appreciate more readily than those who were listening to music at the beginning of the twentieth century. At that time Debussy's works were heard spasmodically and then only in Paris and one or two other centres of music. Apart from the established classical composers the masters who counted at the beginning of the century were Wagner and Verdi, in the field of opera, and Brahms, as symphonist. But they were all respectably dead, and memorialised, by 1901. Wagner died in 1883, Brahms in 1897, and Verdi at the age of eighty-eight, in 1901. Those composers, all of whom Debussy had met, were epochal figures, and their departure conveniently represented the end of an era. The nineteenth century—the grand era of expansion, and optimism, and progress, and prosperity—was over. After which all the apparent values of the age were seen as illusory.

Because operas combine words, music, and action, to represent human emotion and behaviour, they are an index to the values of the society from which they spring and the period to which they belong. In the broad sense nineteenth-century opera was "heroic". Twentieth-century opera, more often than not, is "anti-heroic". Debussy's *Pelléas et Mélisande* is perhaps best described as non-heroic. It is the perfect translation of Maeterlinck's ideas into terms of music and theatre. Maeterlinck, whose text is highly symbolic,

49

pursued the theme that men and women lived in a dream state, that they were not free agents but controlled by unseen forces and circumstances, and that freedom only came with death. In *Pelléas et Mélisande* the story is placed in a Rossetti-like atmosphere, with vaguely medieval castles, wells, lakes, forests, in the imagined kingdom of Allemonde. The atmosphere is set out in the Prelude, where the basic melodic intervals (as in folk music) are shown in dark colouring with the lower strings divided. The woodwind section which follows is not far from the character of the beginning of the Quartet. (Ex. 5) Golaud, grandson of Arkel, King of Allemonde, marries Mélisande—a fugitive from those who had done her many wrongs. Having married Golaud, Mélisande found herself loved by, and in love with, Pelléas, Golaud's half-brother. The situation develops and (predictably) Golaud is displeased. He kills Pelléas, and (predictably) Mélisande, who by now has had a baby, dies. On her deathbed Golaud asks her forgiveness.

Ex. 5

Like every opera libretto this story, although symbolised, can be understood in real life terms. The extent to which it becomes credible depends on the composer, for music is the art that can most directly express the emotional quality of

music is expressiv [margin note]

life that lies hidden behind the veil of words and action. Saint-Saëns once said of Debussy's music that it was "music on needle points"—the music of nervous intensity, of sensations. *Pelléas et Mélisande* is unlike other familiar operas because it is concerned not with action but with the feelings that precede action.

Debussy learned from Wagner the art of presenting the interplay of characters in orchestral terms. He also carried on the general principle of *Leitmotiv*. But he did not, as Wagner did, subordinate the vocal to the orchestral texture. Throughout the opera the vocal lines are of the nature of expressive recitative, sensitive to every inflection of the language. Jean Jacques Rousseau, whose interest in music was considerable, had once hoped that some French musician would come who would realise through the simplicity of recitative the "simplicity and clarity" of the French language. This is what Debussy achieved in *Pelléas et Mélisande*, as the following example, from the beginning of the third act, shows. Mélisande at the window of the castle combs her hair. At first the only sound is that of the harp—the music of silence—and then she sings. (Ex. 6) The character of Mélisande

Dreams 'leitmotiv' from Wag. Rousseau wanted recitative simplicity + clarity of lang. realise [margin note]

Ex. 6

Mes longs che-veux des-cen-dent jus-qu'au seuil de la tour

seems also to be found—musically speaking—in some of the songs, particularly in the 1904 setting of Verlaine's *Les Ingénus*.

Sim. Mélisand style found Verlaines les Ingénus. [margin note]

Now an audience goes to the opera-house primarily in search of entertainment. The opera that departs from the

accepted conventions is unlikely to establish itself immediately as a firm favourite. In the course of time, through the propaganda of those who believe in its values, an opera may break through the barriers of indifference or dislike. So it was with Debussy's opera, which by now is seen as one of the great operas of our time. The fact is, that the way in which Debussy felt about life is the way in which many people now feel. The pioneer in art is more than a pioneer in art.

Pelléas et Mélisande was not produced under the most favourable circumstances. Maeterlinck quarrelled with Debussy over the casting of the part of Mélisande. In the first place it was intended that this should be given to Maeterlinck's wife, but it came to the poet's ears that the directors of the Opéra Comique in Paris had assigned the role to Mary Garden (1877–1967), a Scottish-American who had made a remarkable début in Paris in the title role of *Louise* (an opera by Gustave Charpentier (1860–1956) which Debussy detested). Maeterlinck took it that Debussy had been a party to deceiving him, and he therefore broke off their friendship.

News of this dissension was meat and drink to the general run of Paris opera-goers who enjoyed nothing more than artistic scandal. When *Pelléas et Mélisande* was finally staged, on April 30, 1902, there were noisy demonstrations in the house. Nonetheless a number of the most influential critics wrote of the opera in terms of high praise. It was, said Romain Rolland, "one of the three or four outstanding achievements in French musical history." Other critics complained that Debussy had destroyed rhythm and melody, and that he had produced a decadent work likely to have an adverse effect on public morality. This argument—about art and morality—is still alive; but not any longer in respect of Debussy.

Partly because it had enjoyed the success that stems from scandal, but partly because of its musical quality, *Pelléas et Mélisande* became a box-office draw in Paris. In the years that followed its production Debussy became much more prolific.

A pianist of remarkable insight into the character of the instrument, Debussy began in 1903 to publish those works by which he is best known to music-lovers in general. In 1903 were issued *Estampes* (containing "Jardins sous la pluie"); two years later came the first set of *Images* (containing "Reflets dans l'eau"); and in 1907 the second set of *Images* (containing "Poissons d'or"). In these pieces the colours of landscape, of streams, lakes, rivers, are conveyed by the soft brilliance of Debussy's pianistic style. A master of colour effects he made use of harmonies derived from medieval practices, from the exploitation of old modes and from the "whole-tone" scale, and from the effects of harmony available through discreet and careful use of the sustaining pedal. Each piano piece by Debussy is a new impression. In *Images* impressionism reigns supreme, as this quotation from "Cloches à travers les feuilles" ("Bells across the leaves") shows. Notice the spacing of the sounds, and the extended use of the whole-tone scale, from which quite new, and strange, harmonic clusters arise.

Ex.7

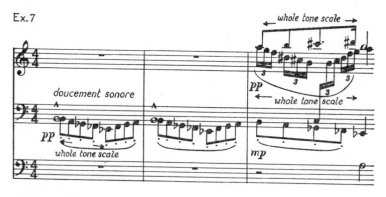

Debussy, the first really to understand what could be achieved through a precise and defined pedal technique, used the piano as he used the orchestra, as a painter's palette. In the *Children's Corner* (1906–8) he added humour to his repertoire. In this collection the range of his influence is shown by the tribute to J. S. Bach indicated in the piece entitled "Doctor Gradus ad Parnassum", and the hint of New Orleans evident in the "Golliwog's Cakewalk". The latter piece was somewhat anticipated by the American composer, Louis Gottschalk (1829–69), in his *Banjo*. In this connection it may be noted that the connection between the

American and the French composer was not quite accidental. Gottschalk had studied in France, was a pupil of Chopin (whom Debussy revered), and deliberately tried to bring to an end the German influences dominating American music.

The connection between Debussy and Chopin is emphasised by the two books of *Etudes* (1915), which were dedicated to the memory of Chopin. Between the *Children's Corner* and the *Etudes* two books of *Preludes*, twelve in each, appeared. The first of these collections contains two other pieces of great popularity—"La Fille aux cheveux de lin" ("The girl with the flaxen hair") and "La Cathédrale engloutie" ("The submerged cathedral"). These works have now passed into the classics of the pianoforte repertoire.

The contrast between the music of Debussy and the pattern of his life is extreme; the one beautifully precise, ordered, and clear; the other uncertain, insecure, and tempestuous. The discrepancy between life and works is similar to that to be found also in the case of Mozart. Both composers saw a vision of an ideal order of which their music was a reflection. But this ideal was far removed from the state in which their personal lives were conducted.

In 1904 Debussy's personal affairs created a scandal. He left his wife (who attempted suicide by shooting herself) for Emma Bardac, the wife of a wealthy financier by whom he had a daughter. In 1905 they were married. A number of songs were dedicated to Mme Bardac (as she was) and the *Children's Corner* to Chouchou, their daughter. Emma Bardac was beautiful, but also intellectual. She was able to provide a congenial background to Debussy's life. She was able to take an active interest in his work and to sympathise with his idealism. Lily was beautiful—but intellectually and artistically had little to offer. So she became a victim of the forces

that drive the lonely artist towards the realisation of his aims.

After the events of 1904–5 — which led to much litigation — Debussy took temporary refuge in England, and it was in Eastbourne in the summer of 1905 that the three wonderful symphonic sketches for orchestra, collectively entitled *La Mer*, were completed. In *La Mer* Debussy shows the sea at different times of day and night, and not only displays its mysterious beauty but also its strength. The whole work is a masterpiece of orchestration. The beginning of the second piece, the "Play of the Waves", even gives some hint of its evocative beauty on paper. One can *see* the waves — across which the two flutes throw a shaft of quiet, but radiant, light. The flutes are in a succession of thirds, illustrating Debussy's exploration of the possibilities of

*summer of [?]
in Eastbourne,
La mer,
see the
stages of
the sea
day-night*

Ex. 8

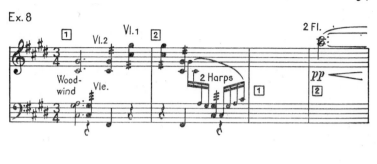

familiar intervals. The same kind of experiment is to be found in the *Etudes* for piano.

La Mer was played in Paris in the autumn, and fierce controversy broke out. This was partly caused by dislike of Debussy and by disapproval of his behaviour. His treatment of Lily Debussy had led to his being deserted even by his best friends, including the poet Pierre Louÿs. Apart—but not very far apart—from this a strong faction of influential musicians and critics considered that Debussy had, as they said, "betrayed" music. The true traditions, it was urged, were maintained by Vincent d'Indy (1851–1931), the most distinguished disciple of the school of César Franck, or even by Charpentier, whom Massenet had proclaimed as his heir designate.

So far as "modern" music was concerned Gabriel Fauré (1845–1924) and Maurice Ravel were strong contenders for high rank. Fauré, the friend of Saint-Saëns, a composer of great delicacy and lyrical sensibility, was an exemplar of formal precision and in no sense revolutionary. Ravel, less elusive in style and expression than Debussy, yet showing certain similarities of outlook, having played his cards better had been able to capture a prominent place much earlier in life than Debussy. Although thirteen years younger he was, in 1905, at least as successful as the older man in the eyes of the musical public.

Very much a lone dog Debussy had antagonised both Fauré and Ravel. The former, who had dedicated his *Bonne Chanson* to Emma Bardac and who—it was said—wished to marry her, had a personal grievance. With the latter it was a matter of professional ethics that caused the rift. In 1902 Ricardo Viñes (1875–1943), a Spanish pianist whose mastery of the works of Debussy and Ravel helped to make them famous, gave the first performance of Debussy's *Estampes*. Not only Ravel noted a similarity between the second piece of the group, "Soirée dans Granade", and Ravel's *Habanera*, also inspired by Spanish impressions and idioms. Ravel's piece had first been played in 1898, and after the performance Debussy had borrowed the music. He had failed to return it.

In 1905 when the Debussy scandal was at its height Ravel was among the many who not only took the side of Lily but took positive steps to help her. Thus, Paris, which had experienced literary feuds and scandals, and had seen the Impressionist school of painting split up into angry and ironical factions, divided into those who were against and those who were for Debussy. Those who supported him even as a musician were very few.

8. *A European Master*

THE STRONGEST SUPPORT for Debussy came from Jacques Durand, his publisher. The firm of Durand had first employed him to make transcriptions for them soon after his return from Rome. At a later point they had contracted with him to publish all his works, and to pay him a monthly allowance on account of what his works might earn. Such a spur was necessary in the case of Debussy, who was a slow worker, and often indolent, and without it it is doubtful how many works would have reached the stage of completion. From time to time Durand needed to prod the composer; many of the piano pieces were the result of such prodding.

By 1907 Durand could reflect with satisfaction that if Debussy was a prophet of doubtful honour in his own country his star was in the ascendant elsewhere.

There was the beginning of a Debussy cult in England, where Henry Wood had conducted *L'Après-midi d'un faune* in 1904, and where a French engineer, J. T. Guéritte, was planning lectures and concerts of French music—particularly about and of Debussy. In 1907 the String Quartet was played in London. In the following year the composer himself visited London, to conduct *L'Après-midi* and *La Mer*, at Queen's Hall. If the critic of *The Times* was bewildered by Debussy's "renunciation of melody" (as were critics all over Europe) there was a strong minority interest in promoting the "new music". In 1909 Debussy was back in London, to conduct *Nocturnes*, and to superintend the rehearsals for the first London production of *Pelléas et Mélisande* at Covent

59

Garden. It had been hoped that Debussy would have conducted at Liverpool where, during a meeting of the British
Musical League, he was represented in one programme. But
he was unable to undertake this.

Even so, by 1909, Covent Garden was hardly in the van
of progress respecting this work, which, more than any other
of his compositions, had made Debussy world-famous. In
1907 it had been given eight performances in Brussels and,
by reaching the Opera House in Frankfurt-Main, had broken

through into the powerfully protected preserves of German opera. In 1908 *Pelléas et Mélisande* was played in Munich, Berlin, New York, and Milan. In the last of these cities, it was mounted in La Scala, the house sacred to the memory and the works of Verdi, and was conducted by Arturo Toscanini. Not being compatible with the popular Italian idea of what an opera should be or do, it caused a riot. But this by many was taken as significant of its importance. So far as New York was concerned the manager of the Metropolitan Opera House, Guilio Gatti-Cassaza, rushed over to Paris to sign for exclusive American rights in the next three operas that Debussy should write. Having made a contract, and having made a substantial advance payment, Gatti-Cassaza was in no way put off by Debussy saying, "Do not forget that I am a lazy composer and that I sometimes require weeks to decide upon one opera [subject] in preference to another."

Certainly at about this time Debussy was pursuing various operatic projects. High on the list of priorities was an opera on the theme of Edgar Allen Poe's (1809–49) fantasy *The Fall of the House of Usher*, on which Debussy worked intermittently for nine years. Other ideas which periodically surfaced were the Don Juan and Tristan legends, and the Romeo and Juliet story, all of which have their established place in the operatic repertory through the scores of other composers.

That Debussy failed to accomplish what he set out to do in this direction is not surprising. As from 1909 he was, symptoms of cancer having shown themselves, under sentence of death. "What sort of a figure will I cut?" he said of himself in respect of a reception he had to attend in London on the occasion of the 1909 Queen's Hall concert. "I shall look like a man condemned to death. I can't get out of it, apparently because of the Entente Cordiale. . . ." Once again we see a musician being used as a piece on the diplomatic chess-board. The *Entente Cordiale*, engineered largely by King Edward VII, signified an alliance between France and Great Britain, as a counter to the growing power of Germany. To some extent, at least, this underpinned a genuine interest in Debussy's music. But when *Pelléas et Mélisande* was acclaimed at Covent Garden on May 21 Debussy was not present to answer the repeated calls for his presence on the stage after the final curtain. He was not well, and resting in his hotel room.

One of the notable figures in European literature at this time was the Italian poet, novelist, and dramatist, Gabriele d'Annunzio (1863–1938). A lover of France, d'Annunzio was a master of the French language, and two of his plays were written in that language. On November 25, 1910, Debussy was surprised to receive a letter from d'Annunzio asking that he should compose incidental music for the sacred "mystery" *Le Martyr de saint Sébastien*. Debussy wrote the music for this play with unusual speed, in a matter of weeks, and was helped in its orchestration by André Caplet (1879–1925), who was to conduct the performance. Before this could take place, however, objections against the work were raised by the Archbishop of Paris. He, influenced by the fact that the play had been put on the Index (of books forbidden by the Church for Catholics), was displeased that the Saint was to be represented by a Jewish actress, Ida Rubinstein, and by what he had heard about Debussy. The poet and the musician issued a dignified statement regretting that the Archbishop, "in a manner that was ill advised, had attacked in his recent decree a work still unknown to him."

Censorship is a dangerous occupation, particularly when the censor is ignorant of the subject of his disapproval.

The score of *Le Martyr de saint Sébastien* is remarkable in showing a less familiar side of Debussy's genius. Much more spacious, much more direct, more formal, and with a certain degree of unaccustomed harshness, the music has a sense of tragedy not otherwise to be so painfully revealed in Debussy. Behind the motiv of "Le Passion", with its gaunt intervals and the imposition of a hard discord in the woodwind, is the spirit of J. S. Bach.

Ex. 9

Le Martyr de saint Sébastien was not a success in Paris, but it was played in the Opera House in Boston (Mass.), in Florence, Venice, Turin, and—on the doorstep of the Vatican—in Rome.

From time to time during these years Debussy, on the whole reluctantly, went abroad to conduct. Apart from a certain sense of gratitude to the English, who had given him as much cause for encouragement as any people, he disliked foreigners. Although he didn't call himself one—largely because of his almost total absorption in his own affairs and in his music—he was a nationalist. He once wrote, "Since every race is endowed with musical instincts, customs, forms and spiritual needs peculiar to itself, frontiers are not purely

E

geographical fictions — to abolish them would be as futile as it is idealistic." But, nonetheless, he owed much to the interest, insight, and encouragement of foreign musicians.

Among those young composers who found Debussy's works a gateway to a new conception of music were Béla Bartók (1881–1945), and Zoltán Kodály (1882–1967), both of whom came to Paris from Hungary to study in the early years of the century. In 1910 Debussy was in Budapest for a performance by the Waldbauer Quartet and was gratified by the reception given to his music. Just prior to visiting Budapest he was in Vienna where he was honoured by a public banquet. During a toast one of the Viennese musicians was rash enough to congratulate Debussy on his "abolition of melody". This was going too far! Debussy rose, and said, "Dear Sir! My music aims at nothing but melody!"

In 1911 Debussy conducted in Turin, but being far from well had to hand over the rehearsal to Vittorio Gui. During this visit he became acquainted with Edward Elgar (1857–1934), and Richard Strauss (1864–1949), neither of whom was temperamentally adapted to an appreciation of Debussy's aims. Elgar succinctly stated that his music "lacked guts". Although he disliked conducting, and was an indifferent performer, Debussy undertook concerts also in Rome, in Amsterdam, and the Hague. In 1913 there were engagements in Moscow and St Petersburg, at the invitation of Sergei Koussevitzky, where Debussy was able somewhat to adjust a lack of balance in Franco-Russian musical contacts. During this visit Debussy renewed acquaintance with Sonia von Meck, who had distinguished herself as a pioneer for women's rights.

For some years the reputation of Russian music had been growing in Paris, while that of French music in the Russian

capitals had remained fairly static. One Russian composer,
Igor Stravinsky (b. 1882), who had made the personal
acquaintance of Debussy in Paris in 1913, thought, however, that Debussy was one of the greatest of then living
composers.

[Handwritten margin note: Rus. pop in Fr but not vice versa. Strav. thoughts highly of Debussy.]

9. *Ballet*

IN 1907, during a period of Franco-Russian friendship, the impresario Sergei Diaghilev arranged an exhibition of works of Russian art in Paris. Emboldened by its success, and with the financial backing of the Russian government, he planned a series of programmes of "Russian music through the ages" which were also successfully given in Paris. Even more successful, however, was the production of Mussorgsky's *Boris Godunov*, with Chaliapin in the title role. A year later Diaghilev, working with the dancer Mikhail Fokin, introduced Paris to the allurements of a new style of ballet. "The Russian Ballet" (although it had no official backing and was a break-away group from the Imperial Ballet) was both successful and provocative.

France was the traditional home of ballet and with the stimulus given by Diaghilev it took on a new lease of life. So far as composers were concerned ballet became the "in" thing. When rumours that Debussy was composing ballet music reached the ears of Gatti-Cassaza he was quick to call on the composer to discuss a further contract—and this despite the fact that nothing had materialized out of the one already partly paid for, in respect of opera. In 1912 Debussy entered the world of ballet from three directions.

An English dancer, Maud Allan, commissioned a brief ballet on an Egyptian subject—*Khamma*. Debussy sketched a piano score, but its orchestration, by Charles Koechlin (1867–1950), was only finished after the composer's death. Another work completed after his death was the children's

ballet *La Boite à joujoux,* which he was invited to write by
André Hellé, a well-known illustrator of children's books.
The orchestration of this "pantomime to the kind of music
I have written for children in Christmas and New Year
albums—something to amuse children, nothing more" was
done by Caplet.

In 1912, Vaslar Nizhinsky, one of the greatest of dancers,
prepared a ballet to the music of *L'Après-midi d'un faune.*
This, which impeded the presentation of Ravel's *Daphnis
and Chloe,* and thus placed another barrier between him and
Debussy, enjoyed an enormous success. Debussy disliked
Nizhinsky's interpretation of the work for artistic reasons.
Other people disapproved it for moral reasons, but notoriety
made it the more attractive to the public. Following this
success Diaghilev commissioned Debussy to write an original
ballet and the result was *Jeux,* to a rather pointless story
about tennis-players! As in *Le Martyr de saint Sébastien* the
music has a sharp edge on it, and at times comes close to
resembling that of Stravinsky, as this passage, sharply dis-
cordant, and in two keys (bitonal), shows.

Ex.10

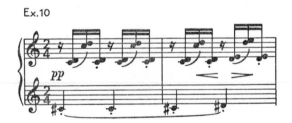

10. *End of an Era*

THE RESEMBLANCE TO STRAVINSKY shown in the dissonances of the previous example reflects the culmination of a Franco-Russian relationship that began with Berlioz. To the Russian nationalists of the 1860's Berlioz appeared as a liberator. Russian musicians of that generation wanted to shake free of German domination. Tchaikovsky also esteemed the French spirit—of clarity and beauty—and as a ballet composer he owed much to the influence of Delibes. Debussy wished to make French music independent of German, and in his early years had before him the scores of Mussorgsky, Borodin, and Tchaikovsky. One of his earliest commissions for Mme von Meck was to make a piano duet arrangement of dances from *Swan Lake*. Stravinsky, who played his *Rite of Spring* with Debussy at the piano from the newly written manuscript, regarded Debussy as he had regarded Stravinsky's predecessors—as an agent of release from the conventions of German musical philosophy.

In 1914 the outbreak of war made a severance from German ideals, in every field, inevitable. Durand, the publisher, projected a new French national edition of classical works to replace the standard German editions. Debussy, irked by not being able to be useful in a more active way, undertook the editing of Chopin's *Waltzes* and *Polonaises*. Under the influence of Chopin he composed his own *Etudes* (*Studies*) which, like those of the earlier master, are technical exercises but, at the same time, more than technical exercises. In these pieces, which range across a wide tract of

fancy and imagination, it is interesting to see how concentration on particular intervals within a single piece opens the door to endless possibilities of harmonic structure. In the third of the *Studies* Debussy deals with the interval of the fourth, and the resulting exploitation of this interval shows a marked similarity to the technique of Bartók.

Ex. 11

pp scherzando

The first rich period of French keyboard music was in the seventeenth century, and the greatest composer of that era was François Couperin (1668–1733). During his last years Debussy reflected on the composers of the Couperin school. "Where," he asked, "are our old claveçinists who had so much true music? They had the secret of gracefulness and emotion without epilepsy, which we have negated like ungrateful children." That, perhaps, serves as a summary of Debussy's own keyboard music.

At the end of his life Debussy planned a series of six sonatas for various combinations of instruments. These were to be studies in different sonorities (cf. the remarks on "Nuages" on p. 46) and also in formal procedures. The first of these sonatas was for cello and piano, the second for flute, viola, and harp, and the third for violin and piano.

The fourth was to have been for oboe, horn, and harpsichord. But this was never written.

At the end of 1916, with no end to the war in sight, oppressed by the feeling of frustration that the war and years of lack of appreciation had brought, Debussy wrote to the Swiss journalist and composer Robert Godet. His letter is a sad and moving farewell, written in the knowledge that death would come soon. "To tell the truth, I go on with this waiting life—waiting-room life, I might say, for I am a poor traveller waiting for a train that will never come again."

On May 5, 1917, Debussy accompanied Gaston Poulet in a performance of the violin sonata. This was his last public undertaking, and his pitiful, emaciated, appearance aroused much sympathy. In the following March long-range guns of the German army bombarded Paris and the inhabitants were driven to take refuge in their cellars. Debussy was too feeble to be carried down from his room. From March 23 to 25 he lay in his bed, with the sound of the guns reverberating through the streets outside. A little more than a hundred years previously a great Austrian musician, Josef Haydn, had heard the guns of an invading army as he lay dying. In his case they were French guns. So we are reminded of two conflicting aspects of European civilisation; on the one hand of the lasting achievements of the great artists, on the other of the destructive forces let loose by national pride and the desire for economic power. We are also reminded that Haydn virtually was the creator of what we know as classical music, and that Debussy, who demolished the tonal system that was its foundation, was a great pioneer of contemporary music.

Debussy died in the evening of March 25, 1918. There

was no notice of his death in the French newspapers, and only a handful of friends at his funeral. In the next year his daughter, Chouchou, died of diphtheria. Emma Debussy died in 1934.

[handwritten margin notes: Died 1918 / 1919 - daughter / died of / Diphtheria / Emma 1934]

Index

References to illustrations are shown in italic type

SET IN 12 POINT CASLON OLD FACE AND
PRINTED IN GREAT BRITAIN
BY THE BOWERING PRESS
PLYMOUTH